by Harry Conroy

LangSyne
PUBLISHING
WRITING *to* REMEMBER

Lang**Syne**

PUBLISHING

WRITING *to* REMEMBER

79 Main Street, Newtongrange,
Midlothian EH22 4NA
Tel: 0131 344 0414   Fax: 0845 075 6085
E-mail: info@lang-syne.co.uk
www.langsyneshop.co.uk

Design by Dorothy Meikle
Printed by Ricoh Print Scotland
© Lang Syne Publishers Ltd 2015

ISBN 978-1-85217-096-7

MacRae

SEPT NAMES INCLUDE:
Maccrae
Maccraw
Maccreath
Macgrath
Macra
Macrach
Macraith
Macrath
Raith

MacRae

MOTTO:
FORTITUDINE.
(With Fortitude)

CREST:
A Dexter hand grasping a sword all proper.

TERRITORY:
ROSS-SHIRE
particularly Wester Ross in
the district of Kintail.

Chapter one:

The origins of the clan system

by Rennie McOwan

The original Scottish clans of the Highlands and the great families of the Lowlands and Borders were gatherings of families, relatives, allies and neighbours for mutual protection against rivals or invaders.

Scotland experienced invasion from the Vikings, the Romans and English armies from the south. The Norman invasion of what is now England also had an influence on land-holding in Scotland. Some of these invaders stayed on and in time became 'Scottish'.

The word clan derives from the Gaelic language term 'clann', meaning children, and it was first used many centuries ago as communities were formed around tribal lands in glens and mountain fastnesses.

The format of clans changed over the centuries, but at its best the chief and his family held the land on behalf of all, like trustees, and the ordinary clansmen and women believed they had a blood relationship with the founder of their clan.

There were two way duties and obligations. An inadequate chief could be deposed and replaced by someone of greater ability.

Clan people had an immense pride in race. Their relationship with the chief was like adult children to a father and they had a real dignity.

The concept of clanship is very old and a more feudal notion of authority gradually crept in.

Pictland, for instance, was divided into seven principalities ruled by feudal leaders who were the strongest and most charismatic leaders of their particular groups.

By the sixth century the 'British' kingdoms of Strathclyde, Lothian and Celtic Dalriada (Argyll) had emerged and Scotland, as one nation, began to take shape in the time of King Kenneth MacAlpin.

Some chiefs claimed descent from

ancient kings which may not have been accurate in every case.

By the twelfth and thirteenth centuries the clans and families were more strongly brought under the central control of Scottish monarchs.

Lands were awarded and administered more and more under royal favour, yet the power of the area clan chiefs was still very great.

The long wars to ensure Scotland's independence against the expansionist ideas of English monarchs extended the influence of some clans and reduced the lands of others.

Those who supported Scotland's greatest king, Robert the Bruce, were awarded the territories of the families who had opposed his claim to the Scottish throne.

In the Scottish Borders country – the notorious Debatable Lands – the great families built up a ferocious reputation for providing warlike men accustomed to raiding into England and occasionally fighting one another.

Chiefs had the power to dispense justice and to confiscate lands and clan warfare produced a society where martial virtues – courage, hardiness, tenacity – were greatly admired.

Gradually the relationship between the clans and the Crown became strained as Scottish monarchs became more orientated to life in the Lowlands and, on occasion, towards England.

The Highland clans spoke a different language, Gaelic, whereas the language of Lowland Scotland and the court was Scots and in more modern times, English.

Highlanders dressed differently, had different customs, and their wild mountain land sometimes seemed almost foreign to people living in the Lowlands.

It must be emphasised that Gaelic culture was very rich and story-telling, poetry, piping, the clarsach (harp) and other music all flourished and were greatly respected.

Highland culture was different from other parts of Scotland but it was not inferior or less sophisticated.

Central Government, whether in London or Edinburgh, sometimes saw the Gaelic clans as

*"The spirit of the clan means much
to thousands of people"*

a challenge to their authority and some sent expeditions into the Highlands and west to crush the power of the Lords of the Isles.

Nevertheless, when the eighteenth century Jacobite Risings came along the cause of the Stuarts was mainly supported by Highland clans.

The word Jacobite comes from the Latin for James – Jacobus. The Jacobites wanted to restore the exiled Stuarts to the throne of Britain.

The monarchies of Scotland and England became one in 1603 when King James VI of Scotland (1st of England) gained the English throne after Queen Elizabeth died.

The Union of Parliaments of Scotland and England, the Treaty of Union, took place in 1707.

Some Highland clans, of course, and Lowland families opposed the Jacobites and supported the incoming Hanoverians.

After the Jacobite cause finally went down at Culloden in 1746 a kind of ethnic cleansing took place. The power of the chiefs was curtailed. Tartan and the pipes were banned in law.

Many emigrated, some because they

wanted to, some because they were evicted by force. In addition, many Highlanders left for the cities of the south to seek work.

Many of the clan lands became home to sheep and deer shooting estates.

But the warlike traditions of the clans and the great Lowland and Border families lived on, with their descendants fighting bravely for freedom in two world wars.

Remember the men from whence you came, says the Gaelic proverb, and to that could be added the role of many heroic women.

The spirit of the clan, of having roots, whether Highland or Lowland, means much to thousands of people.

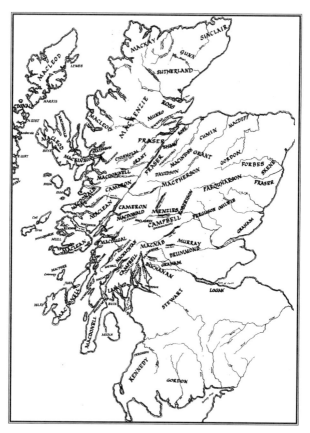

A map of the clans' homelands

Chapter two:

The wild MacRaes

The MacRae clan trace their ancestry back to the Celts and Ireland.

The early members of the clan in the twelfth and thirteenth centuries originally inhabited the lands of Clunes in the district of Beauly in the North East of Scotland before, in the fourteenth century, the clan members moved to the shores of Kintail, in Wester Ross.

The name MacRae means 'son of Grace' or 'son of Good fortune' and is thought to have ecclesiastical origins.

The Irish origins of the clan are traced back to Maurice Macrath, who came to Scotland from Ireland with Colin Fitzgerald, the founder of the MacKenzie clan, and another friend, Gileon na Tuaigh. The trio fled to Scotland following a quarrel in Ireland which became violent when a wedding celebration became too boisterous and blows were struck.

Legend has it that, having arrived at Clunes in the heart of Lovat country, the three friends came upon a would-be assassin attacking Bisset, Lord of Lovat. Maurice Macrath went to Bisset's rescue, slaying the attacker. Following this incident a strong bond of friendship was formed between Maurice and Bisset, and Maurice was invited to settle on the Lovat estates.

Maurice Macrath had four sons, John, Christopher, Duncan and Finlay, all of whom it is believed were born at Clunes, since there was no mention of them having come over from Ireland with their father.

The Lord of Lovat appointed Macrath his chief forester, which led to ill feeling between Lovat's illegitimate son and Macrath, resulting in the exiled Irishman suffering abuse at the hands of the son. This led to Maurice's own son, John, intervening to protect his father and in the ensuing fight Lovat's son was killed. Just as his father had to flee Ireland, John was forced to leave Clunes.

He went to Kintail in Wester Ross where he found lodging in the house of Macauley at Achnagart and eventually married Macaulay's daughter. The couple's first born, Christopher, was the first MacRae to be born in Kintail.

John re-established his father's connection with the MacKenzies, who were in the process of putting down their roots in the west having recently acquired Eilean Donan castle near Dornie, in Ross-shire. John's family became known as Clan Ian Charrich Macrath of Torysich and for around 200 years were a powerful family in the area.

Meanwhile, Christopher, one of Maurice MacCrath's other sons, settled in Brahan, home of the MacKenzies, and his descendants were to be found in Strathgarve, Strathbrennen, and Strathconan. A third son, Duncan, found his way to Argyleshire in the West Highlands and married an heiress of the Campbells of Craignish. His offspring took the Campbell name, thus ending this branch of the Macrath, while the fourth son, Finlay, eventually joined his brother John in Kintail.

John's son, Christopher, was born in 1350 and he in turn also had a son, who he named Christopher, born in 1380. This great-grandson of Maurice Macrath became known as Black Finlay MacRae and he was the progenitor of the Kintail family, the descendants of whom eventually became the keepers of Eilean Donan castle from about 1520.

Such was the bond between the MacRaes and the MacKenzies that as well as being appointed keepers of the MacKenzie stronghold they became known as 'the MacKenzie's shirt of mail'.

One of the MacRae clan's most colourful characters was Big Duncan of the Battle Axe MacRae. He was Black Finlay's grandson and legend has it that during a conflict with the MacDonalds, at the Battle of Park in 1464 near Strathpeffer, Duncan - a huge, wild looking, nineteen year old - found himself on the edge of the battlefield armed with nothing but a rusty old axe.

When asked by another worthy, Red Hector, why he wasn't fighting he replied, looking at the old axe, that when he was given a man's esteem then he would do a man's job. Red Hector caustically informed him that perhaps if he did the job he would earn a man's esteem.

Big Duncan of the Battle Axe accepted this challenge and charged headlong into the midst of the battle and slayed a MacDonald. He seated himself on the body, to survey the scene. Red Hector again challenged him and was told if he only got one man's esteem he would only do one man's job.

Losing patience, Hector told him if he did two men's work he'd get twice the esteem. Hearing this the bold Duncan proceeded to polish off another MacDonald before sitting on the two bodies.

A furious Red Hector threatened the young MacRae to get moving or he would have him to deal with. This threat was enough to stir Duncan into action. He launched himself savagely on the MacDonalds, turning

Clan warfare produced a society where
courage and tenacity were greatly admired

the tide of the battle as he cut down dozens of the enemy.

In the thick of the battle Duncan was confronted by MacLean of Lochbuie, a MacDonald leader who had the reputation of being a deadly enemy in terms of size, strength and courage. However, being clad in chain-mail, he was less agile than big Duncan, who had no armour of any kind.

Duncan seized his chance when MacLean stumbled into a ditch, exposing his neck. The MacRae warrior swung his huge rusty axe and cut the head clean off MacLean of Lochbuie. Seeing their leader cut down in this way the MacDonalds fled, pursued by the MacKenzies and MacRaes through the surrounding hills and glens.

In 1644 the Marquess of Montrose raised the Royal Standard in support of Charles I in the north. The MacRaes joined forces with Seaforth, the MacKenzie chief and again in the Jacobite rebellion of 1715.

Another Duncan at this time fought

under Seaforth. He was also noted for his formidable size and strength and was reputed to have carried a massive stone for a considerable distance before finally laying it down at Auchnagart farm, where it can be seen to this day. This Duncan was a writer of poetry as well as a man of great strength, but sadly he met his death in 1715, along with his two brothers, at the Battle of Sheriffmuir.

His sword was preserved for a long period in the Tower of London, where it was described as 'the great highlander's sword'.

In the subsequent Jacobite rising of 1719 the MacRaes were again involved in the Jacobite cause. The Spanish dispatched under the Duke of Ormonde thirty ships carrying 6,000 troops, but only 300 reached Eilean Donan.

This paltry force was quickly dealt with when, on the 10th of May 1719, three British men-of-war, the Worcester, the Enterprise and the Flamborough sailed up Loch Alsh and set their cannons on Eilean Donan, destroying the stronghold.

The Jacobite rising ended one month later, on the 10th of June, with the defeat of the Jacobites at the Battle of Glen Shiel.

Around this period there was another MacRae descendant, by the name of James, who had left his home in Ayr as a young lad to seek a better life in foreign lands. He returned forty years later a very wealthy man.

To show his gratitude to his cousin, who in his absence had cared for his mother, James provided for the education of his cousin's four daughters and gave them substantial dowries to ensure their marriage to notable men.

The eldest was married to the Earl of Glencairn and received the estate of Ochiltree as a wedding gift from MacRae. To the second he gave the estate of Alva, and her husband became Lord Alva.

The third married the son of Dalrymple, the minister of Ayr, and was given the estate of Orangefield while the fourth married one of his own sons and he was given the lands of Houston in Renfrewshire.

It is perhaps worth noting that the son of the eldest daughter, as the young Earl of Glencairn, was instrumental in boosting the fame of Scotland's national bard Robert Burns when he went to Edinburgh, on the recommendation of his cousin Dalrymple.

This same James MacRae presented to Glasgow in 1734 the town's first statue, the monument to King William III. A monument to the memory of James MacRae himself was erected in the parish of Prestwick near Ayr.

In strange contrast to their warring nature, which led to them becoming known as the 'wild MacRaes', many of the MacRaes, both male and female, showed great aptitude and leanings towards the more gentle pursuits of music and poetry.

From the fifteenth century one of the Inverinate family always held the post of vicar of Kintail. The first vicar, John, was esteemed for his learning, which he had acquired from the monks of Beauly. Another, Farquar MacRae, entered the church and was renowned for his knowledge of Latin.

On his first visit to the Isle of Lewis he is credited with having baptized every resident aged under 40 because they had no resident minister.

Chapter three:

Eilean Donan Castle

Since the history of the MacRaes is so closely linked to Eilean Donan castle it would be wrong not to recount some of the history of one of the most beautiful, if not the most beautiful, castles in the Highlands. It is most certainly the most photographed castle in Scotland.

Eilean Donan possesses an ethereal quality as it is portrayed rising out of the mist on the promontory that marks the meeting point of three lochs, Loch Long, Loch Duich, and Loch Alsh, amidst the romantic beauty of the silent hills.

In reality, however, it was a solid, virtually impregnable stone fortress built not for beauty but for defence against foes. The castle's location was chosen for its strategic value in repulsing marauding Norsemen rather than any aesthetic concern.

There is evidence that the site was used for defensive purposes before the MacKenzie stronghold was built. Remains of a Pict fort were discovered during excavations and these can be seen by visitors to the site.

The name derives from a religious hermit, St Donan, who lived there at the beginning of the seventh century when Celtic monks came to Scotland from Ireland to spread the Christian gospel. The name Eilean Donan means Island of Donan.

After the Picts the first fortified stronghold was built during the reign of Alexander II around 1214. Then, in 1263, Alexander III gave the castle to Colin Fitzgerald, later to become MacKenzie, for services rendered to the King at the battle of Largs when the Vikings were defeated.

John MacKenzie is reputed to have given Robert the Bruce refuge in the castle in the early part of the fourteenth century when he was out of favour with many Clan chiefs and was being hunted by the English.

The Battle of Largs

However when Robert the Bruce's fortunes changed and he established his position as King of Scotland he sent his nephew, Randolph, Earl of Moray, in 1331 to teach those who had shunned him a lesson.

Randolph's crown officer beheaded 50 of the King's foes and displayed their heads atop the battlements of Eilean Donan as a grim warning to others.

After the battle of Glen Shiel the castle lay in ruins for the best part of 200 years until John MacRae-Gilstrap, with the help of Farquar MacRae who had an ambition to restore Eilean Donan to its former glory, rebuilt the fortress (1912-1932). This reconstruction of the castle cost £250,000 and followed old plans, preserved along with other records, in Edinburgh Castle.

Eilean Donan is now owned by the Conchra Charitable Trust, whose trustees have discretion as to its use for special events and on occasion still use the castle.

Unfortunately, despite their rich history, the MacRaes are, sadly, without a Chief. The two rival branches of the clan, the Inverate branch and the Chonchra family, vigorously opposed each other's previous claims and no petition has been lodged in recent years for Chieftainship.

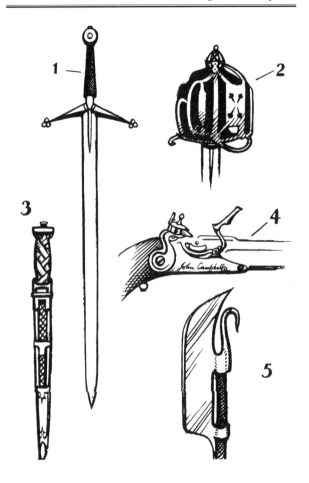

Highland weapons

1)   The claymore or two-handed sword
        (fifteenth or early sixteenth century)

2)   Basket hilt of broadsword
        made in Stirling, 1716

3)   Highland dirk
        (eighteenth century)

4)   Steel pistol *(detail)* made in Doune

5)   Head of Lochaber Axe as carried
        in the '45 and earlier